The Weathering of Igneous Rockforms in High-Altitude Riparian Environments

The Weathering of Igneous Rockforms in High-Altitude Riparian Environments
© John Belk and Cathexis Northwest Press

No part of this book may be reproduced without written permission of the publisher or author, except in reviews and articles.

First Printing: 2020

Paperback ISBN: 978-1-952869-05-1

Cover art by C. M. Tollefson
Designed and edited by C. M. Tollefson

Cathexis Northwest Press

cathexisnorthwestpress.com

The Weathering of Igneous Rockforms in High-Altitude Riparian Environments

By
John Belk

Cathexis Northwest Press

A Sweetheart Melody	11
Mr. Brautigan	12
Lithology I	13
how to grow undone	14
Self-rendered palliative care in a coatroom in New Bethlehem, PA	15
hurt the ones you love	16
how to care for animals	17
The Amazing Flying Feste	18
how to be a hero	19
This Liturgy	20
A Mawkish Popularity	21
Mr. Brautigan (again)	22
in the mission district	23
how to survive a flood	24
Feste at the church of the zombie apocalypse	25
Lithology II	26

Today I	27
how to sleep at night	28
Maundy Thursday	29
Feste at the city park concession stand	30
the oldest words	31
The weathering of igneous rockforms in high-altitude riparian environments	32
Biocrust	33
Mr. Brautigan (the last)	34
Lithology III	35

A Sweetheart Melody
(because we like the way it feels)

Why does anyone cut them
selves on the same glass
repeatedly? Why does a bruise
always shape itself like a tree?
It is always hardest to say goodbye
twice. And why do we start out
green and limber, able to bend
deep into a gale?

Mr. Brautigan

> *I was always waiting for Richard*
> *to grow up as a writer. It was like he*
> *was much more in tune with the trout*
> *in America than with people.*
> —Lawrence Ferlinghetti

I'm curious if you grew tired of
the loneliness and poor weather—
the back-and-forth awkward silences
and being-friends of love.

I think you needed a girl
whose eyes could change color with
the shade of her shirt, and who
wouldn't wonder about clouds so much.
But who's to say for sure
that the company wouldn't curdle?

And who's to say love wouldn't turn
a revolver at your temple
or dangle a fishhook in front of your
lovely, trout-like mouth?

Lithology I

Are river rocks relieved to be discharged
from the pressures of the earth—to only
feel cool water pressed around their forms?
Do they remember their cagemates—the
andesites and diorites that grew beside them
in the white-hot center of everything? Before
they were smoothed in the river, do they still
remember the craggy songs of their youth?

I am all mineral these days: phosphorus and
manganese, made in my own failing image.
I am bad habits, feldspar and hornblende
and sprinklings of self-harm. I am ferrous,
sulphurous, magnetic and spewing forth
bile of earth. I am weathering more every
day. I once knew a song about mountains:
about strength and courage and unfailing love.
I once knew that song by heart.

how to grow undone

I have grown long and slender as
a yew branch shaped into a bow—

shaved down and polished, rubbed
with almond oil and pulled taught

on a wire. I am suffering, blessing,
the deer slain by the bow and

the bow. I have done all that I can.
I could do more.

Self-rendered palliative care in a coatroom in New Bethlehem, PA

So matter of fact about the cutting—
the times she was touched,
the feel of metal, high relief:
x-actos, kitchen knives, the
sharp end of a skewer.

      It was no small thing,
      the telling. The ritual song
      of the flesh.

But it felt small as a wrapper
twisted in nervous resolve—
the marks down her arms leading
to this one story among a million
stories of pain. The sharp wit of
defense that melted like too-early
snow on an open, sunny slope and
left this thing: an egg, an epic,
carapace, scripture, a trailing lyric,
forgotten holy verse in a million
holy verses of pain.

So matter of fact, the history
mapped on skin:
      this was at camp when I found a boxcutter in the supply
      shed; this was from last December; this was a burn from
      a lighter I stole out of Aunt C's purse; this cut was made
      in candlelight when the power was out in October; this one
      looks like a mouse stealing a too-large crumb of bread.

It was no small thing, the telling,
the mollification of flesh, this thing
she held in her hands, this one
story, a million stories, the spine
of the whole gentle world.

hurt the ones you love

go on
they'll forgive you
over and over
blood tossed from
their pores like
spume
spindrift
scud clouds
before a storm

they'll forgive you
in spite of themselves
over and over
they'll forgive you
in the end

how to care for animals

1. feed
2. give water
3. cut off small pieces of your
4. self: a lock of hair, a
5. corner of tongue, a toe
6. conceal the voice raised
7. in frustration
8. always say *I love you* and
9. *daft old man* and
10. *silly silly girl* and
11. *be good, sweet dreams, I'll*
12. *see you in the morning* and
13. always, always *goodnight*

it is blessing to hurt from connection
it is blessing no dog lives long
enough to fail

The Amazing Flying Feste

He thought of joining the traveling circus:
the swinging bars and spinning tops—
everyone would cheer and roar for him.

Men would whistle through fingers,
spewing half-chewed peanut shells
and clapping madly with sausage

hands. Kids would eat nachos and
ice cream and he would hang out between
sets with the fat guy from Frisco.

Women would love him, too. He would be
sex-on-two-feet. He would talk smooth
and show scars and have plenty of lines

at-the-ready to whisper in ears for a kiss—

how to be a hero

      first
try very, very hard
it is normal to feel
ill with kindness
bleeding out

      do not
close your eyes
for fear of
losing or
for fear

      do not
shudder
embrace hurt as
part of caring
as

      part
of knowing
to not cause pain
do not cause
pain

      be styptic
stanch
wounds and dress
with lavender all
cause of woe

This Liturgy
(a leaving off)

It is the ache of a tooth erupting,
a primal hurt from childhood,
thorn that touches bone. Outside
a cat yowls at 3 in the morning.
I cannot tell if it is dying.

We shoulder such burdens but
it is smallness we remember: the
way she took her coffee, the knot I
used for her shoes, the last time we
had lunch (wilted spinach she could
not cut with her teeth).

I savor the smallness—the wind-
worn sculpture of daily routine:
      1. mix 2 tsp instant coffee
      2. feed the cat
      3. sterilize the vanity
      4. remove inner cannula from peroxide soak
      5. help with her morning blouse
I run my tongue across it, this
liturgy, chew it like fat. Sacrament
I haven't performed in years.

The stupidest nooks of our lives
are filled with holy songs: a fried egg
shared, buttermilk for protein, a dying
wish. People are sentimental. People,
like cats, are always walking away.

A Mawkish Popularity

The first time I almost died
was a Sunday. The radiator
sat beside me, seatbelt caught
across my chest—compressed
my heart, stole my wind in trade
and left a mark.

I remember the lakeshore in silence,
pine and cypress three hours from
anything nice. There is a spot along the
road near the long edge of a lake that
can catch the heart off guard—be careful
if you happen on it right.

The last was a seven-year lonely
slow-kill from the inside, buffeted
but measured in gas tanks, bottles,
notes on dog-eared pages in my mind.
She asked if there was anything
about me that wasn't perfect

And I said soft—
be careful of my soft edges
and kindness
and pride.

Mr. Brautigan (again)

> *The problem with learning someone's name*
> *is that a name comes with a person*
> *and an entire life*
> *and yet another beginning.*
> — Ianthe Elizabeth Brautigan

I wonder if things are ever as simple
as making right choices.
In that, I am expert:
the rich mahogany of safe decisions
with ornate leafings of confidence.

But what of splinterings
and second-guesses and
varnishes of regret?
What of paste-wax and carpenter's glue and
happinesses we are sure to never have
       or should have
       or might have soon

as simple as carrying a broken clock
through Tokyo in early June.

in the mission district

in the mission district
a man kneels before the
wooden doors of a church
& cries   he is drunk
he is a workman   he wears
boots like my father
has gossamer hair &
a pipe wrench hung
through a loop of his
belt   he pleads   hands
clasped   his voice wiry
& interrupted   who
can unravel such grief?

it is anguish   our humanity
so full of grace & shame
he pissed himself there
fell asleep on his knees
sobbing a woman's name

how to survive a flood

build a boat
& leave the boat behind
find a whale
& dwell in its stomach
      soft ribbed walls
growing & contracting
like a soul

when the air becomes stale
      build a fire
mingle around its warmth
pray

it tickles   a spark
in the belly
a word in the throat
a person so small & so loud

Feste at the church of the zombie apocalypse

The whole place smelled of cow shit. Everyone—men,
women, children—loaded on grotesque lifted buses

with monster truck tires and window-mounted guns.
On the way to the hotzone they passed a goat petting zoo

and inflated bouncy blob buried in the earth. Children shrieked
with delight as the Pygora named Bubbles nibbled Mother's

sweater. The first zombie was a teenager, maybe 15 and
almost certainly needing the money—padded out in

conglomerate gear: baseball catcher's vest, hockey helmet, ski
goggles, and skate pads strapped to knees. He lumbered from

a pile of tires and Feste opened up, hitting him square
with the third volley. Every moment people are losing

jobs, lovers, entire cities, pets. Liz sez it's an art. People hurt
themselves trying to praise the day. Feste glazes a little, gazes

at the open field of youth. *Fire*, volley, fire—

Lithology II

People pass through orbits, pick up galactic debris—
    hunks of ice, a nickel piece, irradiated zinc.
We accumulate elliptical wards of cobbled-together
    toys: a firetruck for saving, a baseball card
for noise, a bottlecap for under your pillow on nights you
    need the luck. When I was young I stuck stars to
my ceiling and dreamed of endless flight. I lose count
    of people I care for: a girl who heals with touches,
a boy who writes at night, a woman who blankets
    everyone but can only sleep in the light. Why does it
hurt, this hurtling through vastness in inconceivable rush?
    In endless molecular expansion of everything
ever known, we huddle, comfort, something-like-joy,
    something-like-not-alone.

Today I

kissed a friend on the face
made a girl laugh
invented a rhyme
whistled
feared for young children
thought of my mother
held conversation on ancient poems
made bad tea
forgave myself everything
sang at the shifting sky
from the safe side of an open
        door.

how to sleep at night

pillows help—even cheap ones with polyester fill that bunches together like
birds at the end of a branch. I wish I knew the secrets of shutting off a brain.

I wish I knew the secrets of everything: why one cat sleeps in one place until
it feels like moving on; how to turn an eyelid inside out, harmlessly frighten

young children; how to whistle with thumbs. at night I think of kind things—
stupid secrets, whispers so much softer than the vicious questions of the

day. how many bodies can a single bullet pass through before stopping? why
do words translate to mutilated fish? what is violence but another unrighteous

poem scratched into unwilling flesh? at night I tell jokes to fall asleep: did
you hear about the child so soft he could not be hurt? not bullet nor

bludgeon nor gascan flame nor blade nor hatred of men could break
his formless, sensitive, ever-astute and beautiful always bleeding skin.

Maundy Thursday

She hates wet socks—
the stagnant, sticky cotton mist
condensed around her toes.

She has galoshes but
never remembers them.
She even hears the rain

tossing outside—
half-lazy, half-violent—
from heavy eyelids of cloud.

But the boots stay by
the door, a slip of the mind
perhaps.

We are hoping for
a crack in the sky,
for dry ground

and dust and sun—
for a warm place
to rest our shriveled feet.

Feste at the city park concession stand

It needs to be torn down and rebuilt. There
is debate about remodeling—that it would be

cheaper, a better stewardship of taxfunds. In the
desert outside of Las Vegas three women were

beheaded and left, their bodies turned up to the
sun. Feste wonders who misses them: whose hands

are left unheld, what half-empty bottles of lotion
will be found months from now, crusted at the nose

and unfinished. A young boy of valor, no more
than four, hits a ball from a tee, begins to run—

the oldest words

i make soup in the face of sorrow.
it is the same soup each time. it is
all i can think: some ritual of another
life. chickpeas and tomatoes as though
an onion can undo a wound. some
rituals are made of the oldest words:
things grown in soil & in air, broth
& marrow, repentance. it is a thin wire,
grief. we feel it just as deeply with a spoon.

The weathering of igneous rockforms in high-altitude riparian environments

I live in memories:
a careful step through the
laundry room at midnight,
the rough spot on her cheek,
a familiar F-sharp sliding to
blessed resolve, the thornbush
behind the workman's shed
and smell of burning leaves.

I have been careless with
my life more times than
is healthy. I have lived
forever, thought
I would live forever.
And what should I say—

what can be said:
that yesterday was gentle magic—
blown glass and alpine rain.
Today—sunlight and oh,
such beautiful sky.

Biocrust

How fragile are our carefully
curated selves? How stupid?
An entire ecology ground by
careless footfall, baked in noon-
sun, flourished in rains of July.
My heart is on a plate, no, in a
scabbard. My heart is in a common
paper bag. My heart is engulfed
in terrible wine, delicate skin,
coeûr en croute with intricate
folds and pinwheels of daisies
that crisp in the heat. Oh, my
heart. A blooming aster. A wrench.
I found a car in the desert, rusted,
buried barely in the biocrust.
Do not tread here says the sign.
Do not step. Leave no trace except
the colonies of lichen: byssoid,
squamulose, mechanical in their own
organic ways. Leave nothing but the
oldest living things — the ancient,
communal heart of the world worn
on its outer sleeve, respirating together
since the universe flashed itself alive
and bettered itself by knowing you.

Mr. Brautigan (the last)

> *It's beautiful*
> *here by this pond. I wish*
> *somebody loved me*
>   —Richard Brautigan

I want to write a poem that makes everyone love me:
one perfect sonnet to capture every snow melt
homesick champagne full parade-day heart.
It doesn't have to rhyme. In my prayers
I ask for one unimpeachable line, and in dreams
I write holes into moments I know I can't keep.
Each morning I peel back gauze of words like
sympathy and *heartache* and *tilt-a-whirl regret.*
I think of catfish friends and broomsticks and the bedroom
of my first home and where I slept at church camp and I
petition intercession from the anchoress of daybreak
to give me my line — my one perfect line to make
every corner of my mind stop on a hair's edge
of holy, poetic communion and be still.

Lithology III

I buried him under a stone in the rain—
a dull ache of storm in plodding sheets
like funerary linen, fitting and fit
for the day. I marked the stone with
a camp hatchet, ground a crude
circle and slash in the mossed face.
To remember, perhaps remind. To
mark my living in his death, that I—
against odds and worser tendencies
of self—am here.

Acknowledgments

This book would not have been possible without a generous community over the years who have read drafts, talked craft, and been supportive of the word magic that is poetry: Danielle Dubrasky, Sarah Bates, Laura Walker, Robin Becker, Jim Brasfield, Julia Kasdorf, Morgaine Donohue, my family and friends, and so many more who deserve my infinite gratitude and thanks. Thanks to the editorial staff at Cathexis Northwest Press for their vision and care in handling these poems. Thanks also to Cheryl Glenn, who from the beginning held word magic in the same esteem as the rest of my work. And of course, thank you to Cris, whose literal and metaphorical hand helped bring this book to life. Thank you all for aiding in this conjuring, and I hope it does you proud.

Finally, thanks to the editors of the publications where these poems first appeared:

"Self-rendered palliative care in a coatroom in New Bethlehem, PA" in the Worcester Review, vol. 40, nos. 1 & 2, 2019.

"Mr. Brautigan (again)" in Kestrel, no. 42, Winter 2019.

"Mr. Brautigan (the last)" in Kestrel, no. 42, Winter 2019.

"Lithology I" in Comstock Review, Fall/Winter 2019.

"The weathering of igneous rockforms in high-altitude riparian environments" in Cathexis Northwest Press, March 2019.

"Feste at the city park concession stand" in Cathexis Northwest Press, March 2019.

"Today I" in Cathexis Northwest Press, March 2019.

"This Liturgy (a leaving off)" in Levee Magazine, no. 1, Fall 2018.

John Belk is an Assistant Professor of English at Southern Utah University where he directs the Writing Program. His poetry has appeared in *Sugar House Review, Crab Orchard Review, Cathexis Northwest Press, Salt Hill, Kestrel, Worcester Review, Poetry South, San Pedro River Review,* and *Arkansas Review* among others. His scholarship can be found in Rhetoric Review, Rhetoric Society Quarterly, Composition Forum, and edited anthologies. He currently lives in southern Utah among red rocks and stands of juniper.

Also Available From
Cathexis Northwest Press

Something To Cry About
by Robert T. Krantz

Suburban Hermeneutics
by Ian Cappelli

God's Love Is Very Busy
by David Seung

Fever Dream/Take Heart
by Valyntina Grenier

that one time we were almost people
by Christian Czaniecki

The Book of Night & Waking
by Clif Mason

Dead Birds Of New Zealand
by Christian Czaniecki

Cathexis Northwest Press

www.ingramcontent.com/pod-product-compliance
Lightning Source LLC
Chambersburg PA
CBHW030142100526
44592CB00011B/1002